Accounting Made Simpler

Benjamin Wann

Accounting Made Simpler

Copyright © 2023 Benjamin Wann

All Rights Reserved

ISBN: 9798856012490

Table of Contents

	A Note from the Author	5
Ch. 1	The Accounting Equation	7
Ch. 2	The Balance Sheet	11
Ch. 3	The Income Statement	17
Ch. 4	Retained Earnings	23
Ch. 5	Cash Flow Statements	29
Ch. 6	Financial Ratios	35
Ch. 7	GAAP	49
Ch. 8	Debits and Credits	55
Ch. 9	Cash vs. Accrual	71
Ch. 10	Fixed Asset Depreciation	77
Ch. 11	Intangible Asset Amortization	85
Ch. 12	Inventory & Cost of Goods Sold	89
	Conclusion & Wrap-Up	97
	Glossary	99

Accounting Made Simpler

A Note from the Author

Accounting is often viewed as a confusing realm of numbers and technical jargon, seemingly reserved for financial experts and business professionals. However, this perception couldn't be further from the truth. I believe understanding basic accounting concepts is an essential life skill for anyone, which is why I decided to write *Accounting Made Simpler*.

This book is a comprehensive guide that is designed to demystify the world of accounting and make it more accessible to everyone, regardless of background or prior experience. By providing real-life examples and relatable scenarios, I aim to bridge the gap between theory and practice, enabling you to apply accounting concepts confidently in your day-to-day life.

My primary goal is to equip you with the knowledge and confidence to navigate financial matters, whether you're running a business, managing your household finances. Through this book, you'll learn the core principles of accounting in a way that makes sense, without being bogged down by complex terminology.

I hope you find *Accounting Made Simpler* lives up to its title, and I wish you the best of luck on your journey to a financially empowered future.

Thank you,

Benjamin Wann

Accounting Made Simpler

Chapter 1: The Accounting Equation

The accounting equation is a fundamental principle of double-entry bookkeeping, which is the basis for most accounting systems. It represents the relationship between a company's assets, liabilities, and equity. The accounting equation is as follows:

Assets = Liabilities + Equity

Let's break down each component:

1. **Assets:** These are the economic resources a company owns that have the potential to generate future economic benefits. Examples include cash, inventory, buildings, and machinery.
2. **Liabilities:** These are the obligations a company owes to others, such as loans, unpaid bills, and salaries. Liabilities represent claims on the company's assets by external parties.
3. **Equity:** Also known as owner's equity or shareholder's equity, this represents the residual interest in the company's assets after deducting liabilities. In other words, equity is the amount of assets that belong to the company's owners.

The accounting equation ensures that the company's financial statements remain in balance. Every financial transaction affects at least two accounts, with one side increasing and the other decreasing. This ensures that the accounting equation always stays in balance.

Example:

Let's say you start a small business and invest $10,000 of your own money into it. In this scenario, the accounting equation would look like this:

Assets = Liabilities + Equity

$10,000 (Cash) = $0 (Liabilities) + $10,000 (Equity)

Now, let's say you take out a bank loan of $5,000 to purchase additional inventory. The accounting equation would now look like this:

Assets = Liabilities + Equity

$15,000 (Cash + Inventory) = $5,000 (Loan) + $10,000 (Equity)

As you can see, the accounting equation remains in balance. By understanding the accounting equation, you can better grasp the relationship between a company's assets, liabilities, and equity, which is essential for analyzing a company's financial health.

The Accounting Equation - Simple Summary

The accounting equation is a fundamental principle in double-entry bookkeeping that represents the relationship between a company's assets, liabilities, and equity. The equation is as follows:

Assets = Liabilities + Equity

Assets are the economic resources a company owns with the potential to generate future benefits.

A company's liabilities are obligations to others, representing claims on the company's assets.

Equity represents the residual interest in the company's assets after deducting liabilities.

The accounting equation ensures that a company's financial statements remain balanced, with every financial transaction affecting at least two accounts. Understanding this equation is essential for analyzing a company's financial health.

The Accounting Equation - FAQs
1. What is the Accounting Equation?

The accounting equation is a fundamental principle in double-entry bookkeeping that states:

<u>Assets = Liabilities + Equity</u>

It represents the relationship between a company's assets (resources with economic value), liabilities (obligations to others), and equity (owner's interest in the company).

2. Why is the Accounting Equation Critical?

<u>The accounting equation is critical because it provides a framework for recording and organizing financial transactions.</u> It helps maintain the balance between a company's resources and obligations, ensuring that the financial statements are accurate and reliable. Additionally, the equation provides insights into a company's financial position, enabling stakeholders to make informed decisions about the business.

3. How Do Transactions Affect the Accounting Equation?

<u>Every financial transaction affects at least two accounts in the accounting equation.</u> For example, if a company purchases equipment for $5,000 cash, its assets (equipment) increase by $5,000, and another asset (cash) decreases by $5,000. The accounting equation remains balanced because the total value of assets remains the same.

4. What is the Difference Between Equity and Liabilities?

<u>After deducting liabilities, equity represents the owner's or shareholders' residual interest in the company's assets.</u> It consists of the initial investment made by the owners (capital) and the accumulated profits that have not been distributed as dividends (retained earnings).

A company's liabilities are obligations to others, such as suppliers, lenders, and employees. They represent claims on the company's assets by external parties and can be categorized as current (short-term) or non-current (long-term) liabilities.

5. How Can the Accounting Equation Help Assess a Company's Financial Health?

By analyzing the accounting equation, stakeholders can gain insights into a company's financial position, solvency, and ability to meet its obligations. A higher proportion of equity than liabilities indicates a lower financial risk, as the company relies less on external financing. Additionally, comparing the accounting equation over time can reveal a company's financial performance and stability trends.

Chapter 2: The Balance Sheet

A balance sheet is a financial statement that provides a snapshot of a company's financial position at a specific time. It shows the company's assets, liabilities, and equity, which are categorized and listed per the accounting equation:

Assets = Liabilities + Equity

Let's break down each component of the balance sheet:

1. **Assets:** Assets are the resources a company owns that have the potential to generate future economic benefits. They are classified as either current assets (short-term, usually convertible to cash within a year) or non-current assets (long-term, not expected to be converted to cash within a year). Examples of assets include cash, accounts receivable, inventory, buildings, and machinery.
2. **Liabilities:** Liabilities are the obligations a company owes to others. They are classified as either current liabilities (short-term, due within a year) or non-current liabilities (long-term, due after a year). Examples of liabilities include accounts payable, loans, and salaries payable.
3. **Equity:** Equity, known as owner's or shareholder's equity, represents the residual interest in the company's assets after deducting liabilities. It consists of the owner's initial investment and retained earnings (profits not distributed as dividends but reinvested in the company). Common equity components include common stock, preferred stock, and retained earnings.

The balance sheet assists stakeholders such as investors, creditors, and management in understanding the company's financial health and stability. It is a critical tool for evaluating a company's liquidity, solvency, and overall financial performance.

Example:

Here's a simplified example of a balance sheet for a small business:

ABC Company

Balance Sheet

December 31, 20XX

ASSETS

Current Assets:

Cash $10,000

Accounts Receivable $5,000

Inventory $8,000

Total Current Assets $23,000

Non-Current Assets:

Property, Plant & Equipment $30,000

Total Non-Current Assets $30,000

Total Assets $53,000

LIABILITIES

Current Liabilities:

Accounts Payable $6,000

Total Current Liabilities $6,000

Non-Current Liabilities:

Long-Term Loan $10,000

Total Non-Current Liabilities $10,000

Total Liabilities $16,000

EQUITY

Common Stock $30,000

Retained Earnings $7,000

Total Equity $37,000

Total Liabilities and Equity $53,000

In this example, the company's total assets are $53,000, total liabilities are $16,000, and total equity is $37,000. The balance sheet is in balance, as the accounting equation holds true: Assets ($53,000) = Liabilities ($16,000) + Equity ($37,000). Understanding a balance sheet is crucial for assessing a company's financial health and making informed business decisions.

As you can see, the balance sheet provides a snapshot of a company's financial position at a specific point in time. It consists of three primary accounts: assets, liabilities, and equity. However, there are subaccounts within each of those main groupings. Here's a brief explanation of each more detailed account:

Assets:

Assets are the resources owned by a company that have the potential to generate future economic benefits. They are divided into two main categories:

a) **Current Assets:** These are short-term assets expected to be converted into cash or used up within one year or the company's operating cycle, whichever is longer. Examples of current assets include cash, accounts receivable (money owed to the company by customers), inventory (goods available for sale), and prepaid expenses (payments made in advance for future expenses).

b) **Non-Current Assets:** These are long-term assets that are not expected to be converted into cash or used up within one year or the company's operating cycle. Examples of non-current assets include property, plant, and equipment (such as buildings, land, and machinery), long-term investments, and intangible assets (like patents, copyrights, and trademarks).

Liabilities:

Liabilities are the obligations a company owes to others. They are also divided into two main categories:

a) **Current Liabilities:** These are short-term obligations that are expected to be settled within one year or the company's operating cycle, whichever is longer. Examples of current liabilities include accounts payable (money owed to suppliers), accrued expenses (expenses that have been incurred but not yet paid), and short-term loans.

b) **Non-Current Liabilities:** These are long-term obligations that are not expected to be settled within one year or the company's operating cycle. Examples of non-current liabilities include long-term loans, bonds payable, and deferred tax liabilities.

Equity:

Equity, also known as owner's equity or shareholder's equity, represents the residual interest in the company's assets after deducting liabilities. In other words, a portion of the company's assets belongs to the owners or shareholders. Equity has two main components:

a) **Capital:** This represents the initial investment made by the owners or shareholders of the company. It includes common stock, preferred stock, and additional paid-in capital.

b) **Retained Earnings:** This represents the company's accumulated profits that have not been distributed as dividends but have been reinvested in the company or used to cover losses.

Understanding these primary accounts in a balance sheet is essential for assessing a company's financial health and making informed business decisions.

The Balance Sheet - Simple Summary

A corporation's balance sheet displays the company's current financial situation at a specific time. The following equation is used to format balance sheets in compliance with accounting standards: Assets equal liabilities plus equity in the hands of the owners. The assets that are considered current are those that are anticipated to be converted into cash in the next year or less.

By definition, a non-current asset, often known as a long-term asset, is any asset not considered a current asset. The obligations known as current liabilities are those that must be settled financially within the following calendar year. Any liability that is not considered a current liability is considered a long-term liability by default.

The Balance Sheet - FAQs
1. **What is a Balance Sheet?**

A balance sheet is a financial statement presenting a snapshot of a company's financial position at a specific time. It consists of three main sections: assets, liabilities, and equity. The balance sheet is based on the accounting equation (Assets = Liabilities + Equity) and provides insights into a company's resources, obligations, and the owner's interest in the business.

2. **What are the Main Components of a Balance Sheet?**

The main components of a balance sheet are assets, liabilities, and equity. Assets are resources with economic value that a company owns or controls, such as cash, inventory, and property. A company's liabilities are obligations to others, like loans, accounts payable, and accrued expenses. After deducting liabilities, equity represents the owner's or shareholders' residual interest in the company's assets. It includes the initial investment and accumulated profits that have not been distributed as dividends.

3. **What is the Difference Between Current and Non-Current Assets and Liabilities?**

Current assets are short-term resources that a company expects to convert into cash or use up within one year or one operating cycle, whichever is longer. Examples include cash, accounts receivable, and inventory. Non-current assets are long-term resources a company expects to use or benefit from over an extended period, such as property, plant, equipment, and intangible assets.

Current liabilities are short-term obligations that a company expects to settle within one year or one operating cycle, whichever is longer. Examples include accounts payable, short-term loans, and accrued expenses. Non-current liabilities are long-term obligations that extend beyond one year or operating cycle, such as long-term loans and bonds payable.

4. How Can the Balance Sheet Be Used to Analyze a Company's Financial Health?

The balance sheet provides insights into a company's liquidity, solvency, and financial stability. By analyzing financial ratios derived from the balance sheet, stakeholders can assess a company's ability to meet short-term obligations (liquidity ratios), long-term debt repayment capacity (solvency ratios), and overall financial performance (profitability ratios). Comparing balance sheet data over time helps identify trends and potential areas of concern.

5. How Often is a Balance Sheet Prepared?

A balance sheet is typically prepared at the end of each accounting period, such as a month, quarter, or year. Publicly traded companies are required to publish their balance sheets along with other financial statements, like the income statement and cash flow statement, on a quarterly and annual basis. Private companies may prepare balance sheets more frequently, depending on their needs and stakeholders' preferences.

Chapter 3: The Income Statement

The income statement, also known as the profit and loss statement or statement of operations, is a financial statement that shows a company's revenues, expenses, and profits (or losses) over a specific period, usually a fiscal quarter or year. It helps stakeholders understand how a company generates profits and manages its expenses.

Example:

Here's a simplified example of an income statement for a small business.

ABC Company

Income Statement

For the Year Ended December 31, 20XX

Revenues:

Sales Revenue $50,000

Expenses:

Cost of Goods Sold (COGS) $20,000

Gross Profit (Sales Revenue - COGS) $30,000

Operating Expenses:

Salaries and Wages $12,000

Rent Expense $6,000

Utilities Expense $1,500

Depreciation Expense $2,000

Total Operating Expenses $21,500

Operating Income (Gross Profit - Operating Expenses) $8,500

Other Income and Expenses:

Interest Expense $1,000

Total Other Income and Expenses $1,000

Net Income (Operating Income - Other Income & Expenses) $7,500

In this example, the company generated $50,000 in sales revenue and had $20,000 in the cost of goods sold (COGS), resulting in a gross profit of $30,000. After deducting operating expenses ($21,500) from the gross profit, the company has an operating income of $8,500. Finally, after accounting for other income and expenses ($1,000), the company's net income is $7,500.

The income statement provides valuable insights into a company's profitability, cost structure, and financial performance, allowing stakeholders to make informed decisions about the business.

The Income Statement - Gross Profit and Cost of Goods Sold

In the previous example, two key concepts from the income statement are Gross Profit and Cost of Goods Sold (COGS). Let's break down each concept for beginners:

Cost of Goods Sold (COGS):

COGS represents the total cost of producing or acquiring a company's goods sold during a specific period. It includes costs such as raw materials, direct labor, and manufacturing overhead directly related to the production process. COGS does not include indirect expenses like marketing, sales, and administrative costs.

For example, if a company purchases raw materials for $10,000, spends $5,000 on direct labor to manufacture the goods, and incurs $5,000 in manufacturing overhead costs (e.g., factory rent, utilities, and equipment depreciation), the COGS would be $20,000.

Gross Profit:

Gross Profit is the difference between a company's total sales revenue and COGS. It shows how much money a company generates from its core business operations, excluding operating expenses and other income or expenses.

To calculate Gross Profit, you subtract the COGS from the sales revenue:

Gross Profit = Sales Revenue - COGS

In the example provided, the company's sales revenue is $50,000, and the COGS is $20,000. Therefore, the Gross Profit is:

Gross Profit = $50,000 (Sales Revenue) - $20,000 (COGS) = $30,000

Gross Profit provides a snapshot of a company's ability to generate profit from its core business activities before accounting for operating expenses, taxes, and other costs. It helps stakeholders assess the company's efficiency in turning raw materials and labor into profitable products or services. A higher gross profit margin (Gross Profit / Sales Revenue) indicates that a company is more efficient in its production process and has better control over its costs.

The Income Statement - Simple Summary

A company's quarterly or annual **income statement** shows its revenues, expenses, and profits (or losses). It helps stakeholders evaluate the company's financial performance and comprehend its profit and spending management.

Cost of Goods Sold (COGS) is the entire cost of manufacturing or acquiring goods a company sells over a period. COGS contains production-related raw commodities, direct labor, and manufacturing overhead. Marketing, sales, and administrative charges are excluded.

Gross Profit is sales revenue minus COGS. It shows a company's main business revenue before operating expenses and other income or expenses. Gross Profit shows stakeholders how well a company turns raw supplies and labor into profit. Higher gross profit margins suggest better production cost control and efficiency.

In summary, the **Income Statement** shows a company's financial performance, whereas COGS and Gross Profit reveal its key business activities' efficiency and profitability.

The Income Statement - FAQs

1. What is an Income Statement?

An income statement, also known as a profit and loss statement or statement of operations, is a financial statement that shows a company's revenues, expenses, and net income (profit or loss) over a specific period, usually a fiscal quarter or year. It helps stakeholders understand how a company generates profits and manages its expenses.

2. What are the Main Components of an Income Statement?

The main components of an income statement are revenues, expenses, and net income. Revenues represent the money a company earns from its business activities, such as sales of products or services. Expenses are the costs incurred to generate those revenues, including the cost of goods sold (COGS), operating expenses, and other expenses like interest and taxes. Net income is the difference between revenues and expenses, indicating the company's profit or loss for the period.

3. What is the Difference Between Gross Profit and Operating Income?

Gross profit is the difference between a company's total sales revenue and COGS. It shows how much money a company generates from its core business operations before accounting for operating expenses and other income or expenses. Operating income, also known as operating profit or operating earnings, is the difference between gross profit and operating expenses. It reflects the company's profitability from its core operations, excluding non-operating items like interest and taxes.

4. **How Can the Income Statement be Used to Analyze a Company's Financial Performance?**

The income statement provides insights into a company's profitability, cost structure, and financial performance. By analyzing financial ratios derived from the income statement, such as gross profit margin, operating margin, and net profit margin, stakeholders can assess a company's efficiency in generating profits and managing expenses. Comparing income statement data over time helps identify trends and potential areas of concern or improvement.

5. **How Often Is an Income Statement Prepared?**

An income statement is typically prepared at the end of each accounting period, such as a month, quarter, or year. Publicly traded companies must publish their income statements along with other financial statements, like the balance sheet and cash flow statement, on a quarterly and annual basis. Private companies may prepare income statements more frequently, depending on their needs and stakeholders' preferences.

Chapter 4: Retained Earnings

The Statement of Retained Earnings, also known as the Statement of Owner's Equity or the Equity Statement, is a financial statement that shows the changes in a company's retained earnings over a specific period, typically a fiscal quarter or year. Retained earnings are the portion of a company's net income that is not distributed as dividends but is kept by the company to reinvest in the business or pay off debts.

The statement of retained earnings serves a purpose that is analogous to that of a bridge between the income statement and the balance sheet. It does this by taking data from the income statement and feeding it to the balance sheet. The final step in the process of preparing an income statement is to calculate the net income of the company:

Example:

Here's a simple example of a Statement of Retained Earnings to help illustrate the concept.

ABC Company

Statement of Retained Earnings

For the Year Ended December 31, 2022

1. Beginning Retained Earnings (January 1, 2022): $10,000
2. Net Income for the year: $8,000
3. Dividends paid during the year: $2,000
4. Ending Retained Earnings (December 31, 2022): $16,000

The Statement of Retained Earnings provides insights into a company's ability to reinvest profits, manage dividends, and grow its business. It helps stakeholders understand how a company's earnings are allocated between reinvestment and shareholder distributions.

The statement starts with the beginning retained earnings balance, which is the amount of retained earnings at the start of the period (January 1, 2022) - in this case, $10,000.

Next, the company's net annual income is added to the beginning retained earnings. In this example, ABC Company earned a net income of $8,000 during the year.

Then, any dividends paid to shareholders during the period are subtracted from the total. ABC Company paid out $2,000 in dividends during the year.

Finally, the ending retained earnings balance is calculated by adding the net income to the beginning retained earnings and subtracting the dividends paid. In this example, the ending retained earnings balance for ABC Company on December 31, 2022, is $16,000.

Dividends: Not an Expense! When people are beginning to learn accounting, one of the most common mistakes they make is recording dividend payments as costs. Given that they are cash payments made by the company to another party, it is true that they do have many of the same characteristics as expenses.

On the other hand, dividends are a distribution of profits rather than cash payments like many other types of payments (as opposed to expenses, which reduce profits). The dividend payments do not appear on the income statement because they are not included in the calculation of the net income. On the other hand, they will be shown on the statement of retained earnings.

Retained Earnings are not the same as cash. The definition of retained earnings, which is the sum of a company's undistributed profits over the entire existence of the company, makes it sound as if a company's Retained Earnings balance must be sitting around somewhere as cash in a checking or savings account. However, this is not the case. Retained earnings are the sum of a company's undistributed profits over the entire existence of the company.

On the other hand, it is highly unlikely that this is the case. It is not necessary to assume that a company has not put its profits back into the hands of its owners for the company to have put them to use for some other purpose. For example, a significant portion of a company's profits are typically re-invested in the expansion of the business by purchasing additional equipment for production or additional inventory for sale.

Retained Earnings - Simple Summary

The **Statement of Retained Earnings** tracks the changes in retained earnings over a specific period, such as a quarter or a year.

Retained earnings represent the portion of a company's net income that is not distributed as dividends but is kept by the company to reinvest in the business or pay off debts. It is an essential component of a company's equity and is reported on the balance sheet.

This statement helps stakeholders understand how a company allocates its earnings between reinvestment and shareholder distributions, providing insights into its ability to grow and manage its financial resources.

Retained Earnings - Retained Earnings FAQs
1. What are Retained Earnings?

<u>Retained earnings are the accumulated net income a company has earned over time that has not been distributed as dividends to shareholders.</u> They represent the profits a company chooses to reinvest in the business or use to pay off debts rather than distributing to owners or shareholders.

2. Where Can I Find Retained Earnings on a Company's Financial Statements?

Retained earnings are reported on a company's balance sheet under the equity section. The Statement of Retained Earnings, a separate financial statement, shows the changes in retained earnings over a specific period, typically a fiscal quarter or year.

3. How Do Retained Earnings Impact a Company's Financial Position?

Retained earnings impact a company's financial position by contributing to its equity, which is the owner's or shareholders' residual interest in the company's assets after deducting liabilities. A higher retained earnings balance indicates that a company has reinvested more of its profits, which can lead to increased growth, reduced debt, and improved financial stability over time.

4. How are Retained Earnings Calculated?

Retained earnings are calculated by adding the net income to the beginning retained earnings balance and subtracting any dividends paid to shareholders during the period. The formula is:

Ending Retained Earnings = Beginning Retained Earnings + Net Income - Dividends Paid

5. What is the Significance of Negative Retained Earnings?

Negative retained earnings, or accumulated deficits, occur when a company's cumulative net losses and/or dividend payments exceed its net income. This may indicate that the company is experiencing financial difficulties, as it is not generating enough profits to cover its expenses and shareholder distributions.

However, negative retained earnings do not necessarily imply that a company is on the verge of bankruptcy, as it may be experiencing temporary challenges or investing heavily in growth opportunities. Analyzing other financial statements and ratios can provide a more comprehensive understanding of the company's financial health.

Accounting Made Simpler

Chapter 5: Cash Flow Statements

The Cash Flow Statement, also known as the Statement of Cash Flows, is a financial statement showing a company's cash inflows and outflows over a specific period, usually a fiscal quarter or year. It helps stakeholders understand how a company generates and uses cash in its operations, investments, and financing activities. The Cash Flow Statement is divided into three sections: operating activities, investing activities, and financing activities.

Let's go over the three main activities of cash flows:

1. **Operating Activities:** These include cash inflows and outflows related to the company's core business operations, such as sales revenue and payments for salaries, rent, and taxes. In this example, the net cash from operating activities is $5,800.
2. **Investing Activities:** These include cash inflows and outflows related to investments in long-term assets, such as property, plant, and equipment. In this example, the net cash from investing activities is ($2,000), indicating a cash outflow for purchasing equipment.
3. **Financing Activities:** These include cash inflows and outflows related to a company's financing activities, such as issuing stock, borrowing money, or paying dividends. In this example, the net cash from financing activities is $1,500.

Example:

Here's a simple example of a Cash Flow Statement to help illustrate the concept.

XYZ Company

Cash Flow Statement

For the Year Ended December 31, 2022

Cash Flows from Operating Activities:

Net Income: $5,000

Depreciation Expense: $1,000

Increase in Accounts Receivable: ($500)

Increase in Accounts Payable: $300

Net Cash from Operating Activities: $5,800

Cash Flows from Investing Activities:

Purchase of Equipment: ($2,000)

Net Cash from Investing Activities: ($2,000)

Cash Flows from Financing Activities:

Issuance of Stock: $3,000

Dividends Paid: ($1,500)

Net Cash from Financing Activities: $1,500

Net Increase in Cash: $5,300

Beginning Cash Balance: $2,000

Ending Cash Balance: $7,300

Finally, the net increase in cash ($5,300) is calculated by summing the cash flows from operating, investing, and financing activities.

The ending cash balance ($7,300) is determined by adding the net increase in cash to the beginning cash balance ($2,000).

The Cash Flow Statement provides insights into a company's liquidity, cash management, and overall financial health. It helps stakeholders assess how effectively a company generates cash to fund its operations, investments, and shareholder distributions.

Cash Flow Statement vs. Income Statement

The Cash Flow and Income Statements are essential financial statements, but they serve different purposes and provide distinct insights into a company's financial performance.

Cash Flow Statement: This statement shows the inflows and outflows of cash for a company over a specific period. It is divided into three sections: operating, investing, and financing. The Cash Flow Statement provides insights into a company's liquidity, cash management, and ability to generate cash from its operations, investments, and financing. It helps stakeholders understand how a company uses its cash and whether it has enough to meet its obligations and fund future growth.

Income Statement: Also known as the Profit and Loss Statement, this statement shows a company's revenues, expenses, and net income (profit or loss) over a specific period. It provides insights into a company's profitability, cost structure, and financial performance. The Income Statement helps stakeholders understand how a company generates its profits and manages its expenses. It calculates various financial ratios to assess the company's efficiency and effectiveness in generating profits.

In summary, the Cash Flow Statement focuses on the actual cash inflows and outflows during a period, while the Income Statement focuses on the company's revenues and expenses to determine its profitability. Both statements are crucial for stakeholders to analyze a company's financial health and make informed decisions.

Cash Flow Statements - Simple Summary

The income and cash flow statements are different because they present transactions at various times. The fact that many transactions on the cash flow statement are not on the income statement distinguishes it from an income statement.

Cash flow from operating activities includes most cash transactions included in cash flow from operating activities.

Cash flows from investing include cash flows related to long-term assets like real estate, machinery, and equipment and cash flows related to a company's investments in financial securities.

The company's cash flows from financing activities also cover cash exchanges with its owners or creditors.

Cash Flow Statements – FAQs
1. What is the Purpose of the Cash Flow Statement?

The purpose of the Cash Flow Statement is to provide information about a company's cash inflows and outflows during a specific period. It helps stakeholders understand how a company generates and uses cash in its operations, investments, and financing activities. It also gives insights into the company's liquidity, cash management, and financial health.

2. How is the Cash Flow Statement Different from the Income Statement?

The Cash Flow Statement focuses on the actual cash inflows and outflows during a period, whereas the Income Statement focuses on the company's revenues and expenses to determine its profitability. The Income Statement shows a company's financial performance regarding profits and losses. At the same time, the Cash Flow Statement reveals how the company generates and uses cash to support its operations, investments, and financing.

3. What are the Three Sections of the Cash Flow Statement?

The Cash Flow Statement is divided into three sections: operating activities, investing activities, and financing activities. Operating activities represent cash flows related to the company's core business operations. Investing activities involve cash flows related to investments in long-term assets, such as property, plant, and equipment. Financing activities include cash flows related to the company's financing activities, such as issuing stock, borrowing money, or paying dividends.

4. Why is the Cash Flow Statement Important for a Company's Financial Analysis?

The Cash Flow Statement is essential for a company's financial analysis because it shows whether it can generate enough cash to meet its obligations, fund its operations, and invest in growth opportunities. It also helps stakeholders assess a company's liquidity, cash management, and financial health. By analyzing the Cash Flow Statement, stakeholders can gain insights into a company's ability to generate cash and make informed decisions about the company's future prospects.

5. Can a Company Be Profitable but Have Negative Cash Flow?

Yes, a company can be profitable (as shown on the Income Statement) but still have negative cash flow (as shown on the Cash Flow Statement). This situation can occur when a company's revenues are not yet received as cash (e.g., sales on credit) or when the company is investing heavily in growth opportunities or experiencing temporary cash management challenges. Analyzing the Income and Cash Flow Statement to understand a company's overall financial health is essential.

Chapter 6: Financial Ratios

Financial ratios are useful tools to analyze and compare a company's financial performance and health. They are calculated using information from a company's financial statements, such as the balance sheet and income statement. Financial ratios are typically categorized into five main groups: liquidity, solvency, profitability, efficiency, and market value ratios.

Financial Ratios - Liquidity Ratios

Let's begin by examining a common financial ratio from the liquidity category for beginners.

The ease with which an organization can meet its short-term financial obligations is one of the primary purposes for calculating a company's liquidity ratio. Regarding liquidity ratios, generally, a higher number indicates a better situation.

Current Ratio:

The current ratio is a liquidity ratio that measures a company's ability to pay its short-term obligations using its short-term assets. A higher current ratio indicates a better ability to cover short-term liabilities, while a lower ratio may indicate potential liquidity problems.

Formula: Current Ratio = Current Assets / Current Liabilities

Example:

XYZ Company's Balance Sheet:

Current Assets: $100,000

Current Liabilities: $50,000

Current Ratio Calculation:

Current Ratio = $100,000 (Current Assets) / $50,000 (Current Liabilities) = 2

In this example, XYZ Company's current ratio is 2, meaning it has two times the amount of current assets to cover its current liabilities. This indicates the company has sufficient short-term assets to meet its short-term obligations, suggesting good liquidity.

For beginners, it's important to note that financial ratios should be used in conjunction with other ratios and financial analysis tools to gain a comprehensive understanding of a company's financial health. Comparing a company's financial ratios with industry benchmarks and competitors can provide valuable insights into its relative performance and potential areas for improvement.

The Quick Ratio

The Quick Ratio, or the Acid-Test Ratio, is a liquidity ratio that measures a company's ability to pay its short-term obligations using its most liquid assets. It is more conservative than the Current Ratio because it excludes inventory from the calculation, which might not be easily converted into cash in the short term.

Formula: Quick Ratio = (Current Assets - Inventory) / Current Liabilities

Example:

XYZ Company's Balance Sheet:

Current Assets: $100,000

Inventory: $30,000

Current Liabilities: $50,000

Quick Ratio Calculation:

Quick Ratio = ($100,000 (Current Assets) - $30,000 (Inventory)) / $50,000 (Current Liabilities) = 1.4

In this example, XYZ Company's quick ratio is 1.4, meaning it has 1.4 times the amount of its most liquid assets to cover its current liabilities. This indicates that the company can quickly convert its liquid assets into cash to meet its short-term obligations without relying on the sale of inventory.

For beginners, it's important to remember that the Quick Ratio provides a more stringent assessment of a company's liquidity than the Current Ratio. Comparing the Quick Ratio with industry benchmarks and competitors can offer valuable insights into a company's short-term financial health and its ability to manage unexpected expenses or downturns in the business.

Financial Ratios - Profitability Ratios

Profitability ratios are financial metrics that help assess a company's ability to generate profits relative to its sales, assets, or equity. They are essential indicators of a company's financial performance and efficiency. There are several profitability ratios, but we'll focus on three key variants: Gross Profit Margin, Operating Profit Margin, and Net Profit Margin.

Gross Profit Margin:

Gross Profit Margin measures the percentage of revenue remaining after subtracting the cost of goods sold (COGS). It indicates the efficiency of a company in producing and selling its products.

Formula: Gross Profit Margin = (Gross Profit / Revenue) * 100

Operating Profit Margin:

Operating Profit Margin measures the percentage of revenue remaining after subtracting the cost of goods sold (COGS) and operating expenses. It indicates the efficiency of a company in managing its core business operations.

Formula: Operating Profit Margin = (Operating Profit / Revenue) * 100

Net Profit Margin:

Net Profit Margin measures the percentage of revenue remaining after subtracting all expenses, including taxes and interest. It indicates the overall profitability of a company.

Formula: Net Profit Margin = (Net Profit / Revenue) * 100

Example:

XYZ Company's Income Statement:

Revenue: $500,000

Cost of Goods Sold (COGS): $300,000

Operating Expenses: $100,000

Interest and Taxes: $50,000

Calculations:

Gross Profit = $500,000 (Revenue) - $300,000 (COGS) = $200,000

Operating Profit = $200,000 (Gross Profit) - $100,000 (Operating Expenses) = $100,000

Net Profit = $100,000 (Operating Profit) - $50,000 (Interest and Taxes) = $50,000

Gross Profit Margin = ($200,000 / $500,000) * 100 = 40%

Operating Profit Margin = ($100,000 / $500,000) * 100 = 20%

Net Profit Margin = ($50,000 / $500,000) * 100 = 10%

In this example, XYZ Company has a Gross Profit Margin of 40%, Operating Profit Margin of 20%, and Net Profit Margin of 10%. These ratios indicate the company's efficiency in generating profits at different stages of its operations.

For beginners, it's essential to use profitability and other financial ratios and analysis tools to understand a company's overall financial performance. Comparing a company's profitability ratios with industry benchmarks and competitors can provide valuable insights into its relative performance and potential areas for improvement.

Return on Assets & Equity

Return on Assets (ROA) and Return on Equity (ROE) are essential profitability ratios used to assess a company's efficiency in generating returns from its investments.

Return on Assets (ROA):

ROA measures a company's ability to generate profits from its total assets. It indicates how efficiently a company uses its assets to generate net income.

Formula: ROA = Net Income / Total Assets

Return on Equity (ROE):

ROE measures a company's ability to generate profits from its shareholders' equity. It indicates how efficiently a company uses the investments made by its shareholders to generate net income.

Formula: ROE = Net Income / Shareholders' Equity

Example:

XYZ Company's financial data:

Net Income: $50,000

Total Assets: $250,000

Shareholders' Equity: $150,000

Calculations:

ROA = $50,000 (Net Income) / $250,000 (Total Assets) = 0.20 or 20%

ROE = $50,000 (Net Income) / $150,000 (Shareholders' Equity) = 0.333 or 33.3%

In this example, XYZ Company has a ROA of 20%, indicating that it generates $0.20 in net income for every dollar invested in its assets. It has an ROE of 33.3%, which generates $0.333 in net income for every dollar of shareholders' equity.

For beginners, it's important to note that ROA and ROE should be used in conjunction with other financial ratios and analysis tools to understand a company's overall financial performance comprehensively. Comparing a company's ROA and ROE with industry benchmarks and competitors can provide valuable insights into its relative efficiency and effectiveness in generating returns from its assets and equity.

Financial Ratios - Financial Leverage Ratios

Financial leverage ratios assess a company's debt levels and ability to meet its financial obligations. These ratios provide insights into the risk associated with a company's capital structure. Two key financial leverage ratios are the Debt Ratio and the Debt-to-Equity Ratio.

Debt Ratio:

The Debt Ratio measures the proportion of a company's debt-financed assets. It indicates the financial risk associated with a company's capital structure, as a higher ratio suggests more reliance on borrowed funds.

Formula: Debt Ratio = Total Debt / Total Assets

Debt-to-Equity Ratio:

The Debt-to-Equity Ratio measures the proportion of a company's debt compared to its shareholders' equity. It indicates the relative contributions of creditors and shareholders in financing a company's assets. A higher ratio suggests more reliance on borrowed funds and potential financial risk.

Formula: Debt-to-Equity Ratio = Total Debt / Shareholders' Equity

Example:

XYZ Company's financial data:

Total Assets: $500,000

Total Debt: $200,000

Shareholders' Equity: $300,000

Calculations:

Debt Ratio = $200,000 (Total Debt) / $500,000 (Total Assets) = 0.4 or 40%

Debt-to-Equity Ratio = $200,000 (Total Debt) / $300,000 (Shareholders' Equity) = 0.666 or 66.6%

In this example, XYZ Company has a Debt Ratio of 40%, indicating that 40% of its assets are financed by debt. It has a Debt-to-Equity Ratio of 66.6%, suggesting that the company has $0.666 in debt for every dollar of equity.

For beginners, it's important to use financial leverage, other financial ratios, and analysis tools to comprehend and understand financial risk and capital structure. Comparing a company's financial leverage ratios with industry benchmarks and competitors can provide valuable insights into its relative risk exposure and financing strategy.

Benefits and Disadvantages of Financial Leverage

Financial leverage is using debt to finance a company's assets to enhance the potential return on equity. While financial leverage can lead to higher returns for shareholders, it also comes with risks. Here are the benefits and disadvantages of financial leverage, along with examples for beginners:

Benefits of Financial Leverage:

Enhanced Returns: When a company uses borrowed funds to finance investments that generate a higher return than the interest cost, it can boost shareholders' returns. This is because the company can earn more from the investment than the interest expense, increasing the net income available for shareholders.

Example: A company borrows $1 million at a 5% interest rate and invests it in a project that yields an 8% return. The company earns an additional 3% return (8% - 5%) on the borrowed funds, increasing its shareholders' overall res shareholders.

Tax Benefits: Interest payments on debt are tax-deductible, which can help reduce a company's tax liability. This can result in higher after-tax income for the company and its shareholders.

Example: A company has $100,000 in taxable income and $20,000 in interest expense. The company's taxable income is reduced to

$80,000 ($100,000 - $20,000) due to the interest expense deduction, which lowers its tax liability.

Disadvantages of Financial Leverage:

Increased Risk: Using financial leverage increases a company's fixed interest payments, making it more vulnerable to economic downturns and fluctuations in its income. The inability to meet interest payments can lead to bankruptcy.

Example: A company with a high debt load may face difficulty meeting its interest payments during an economic downturn, putting its financial stability at risk and potentially leading to bankruptcy.

Dilution of Ownership: Borrowing funds may require a company to issue more shares to raise additional capital, which can dilute existing shareholders' ownership and control.

Example: A company issues additional shares to raise capital for debt repayment, decreasing the ownership percentage for existing shareholders.

For beginners, it's important to understand that financial leverage can be a double-edged sword. While it can potentially boost shareholder returns, it also carries increased risks. The key to successful financial leverage is to use it judiciously, ensuring that the benefits outweigh the potential risks.

Financial Ratios - Asset Turnover Ratios

Asset Turnover Ratio is a financial efficiency ratio that measures a company's ability to generate revenue from its assets. It indicates how effectively a company uses its assets to produce sales.

Inventory Turnover, Average Inventory, Receivables Turnover, and Average Collection Period are essential ratios to assess a company's efficiency in managing its inventory and receivables. Here's a brief explanation of each with examples:

Inventory Turnover:

Inventory Turnover measures how often a company sells and replaces its inventory within a specific period. A higher ratio indicates better inventory management and sales efficiency.

Formula: Inventory Turnover = Cost of Goods Sold (COGS) / Average Inventory

Average Inventory:

Average Inventory is the midpoint inventory level between the beginning and ending inventory for a specific period. It's used to calculate the Inventory Turnover ratio.

Formula: Average Inventory = (Beginning Inventory + Ending Inventory) / 2

Receivables Turnover:

Receivables Turnover measures how efficiently a company collects its outstanding receivables. A higher ratio suggests better credit management and collection efficiency.

Formula: Receivables Turnover = Net Credit Sales / Average Accounts Receivable

Average Collection Period:

The Average Collection Period measures the days a company takes to collect customer payments. A shorter period indicates better credit management and collection efficiency.

Formula: Average Collection Period = 365 days / Receivables Turnover

Example:

XYZ Company's financial data:

COGS: $300,000

Beginning Inventory: $60,000

Ending Inventory: $80,000

Net Credit Sales: $400,000

Beginning Accounts Receivable: $30,000

Ending Accounts Receivable: $40,000

Calculations:

Average Inventory = ($60,000 + $80,000) / 2 = $70,000

Inventory Turnover = $300,000 (COGS) / $70,000 (Average Inventory) = 4.29 times

Average Accounts Receivable = ($30,000 + $40,000) / 2 = $35,000

Receivables Turnover = $400,000 (Net Credit Sales) / $35,000 (Average Accounts Receivable) = 11.43 times

Average Collection Period = 365 days / 11.43 (Receivables Turnover) = 31.9 days

In this example, XYZ Company has an Inventory Turnover of 4.29, indicating that it sells and replaces its inventory about 4.29 times per year. The company's Receivables Turnover is 11.43, suggesting efficient credit management, and its Average Collection Period is approximately 31.9 days, indicating that it takes about 32 days to collect customer payments.

For beginners, these ratios provide insights into a company's operational efficiency and should be used with other financial ratios and analysis tools to assess overall financial performance. Comparing these ratios with industry benchmarks and competitors can provide valuable insights into the company's relative efficiency in managing its inventory and receivables.

Formula: **Asset Turnover Ratio = Net Sales / Average Total Assets**

Where: Net Sales is the revenue generated from the company's primary operations, excluding any returns, allowances, or discounts.

Average Total Assets is the average of the company's total assets at the beginning and end of the accounting period.

Example:

XYZ Company's financial data:

Net Sales: $600,000

Beginning Total Assets: $400,000

Ending Total Assets: $500,000

Calculations:

Average Total Assets = ($400,000 + $500,000) / 2 = $450,000

Asset Turnover Ratio = $600,000 (Net Sales) / $450,000 (Average Total Assets) = 1.33

In this example, XYZ Company has an Asset Turnover Ratio of 1.33, which generates $1.33 in net sales for every dollar invested in its assets.

For beginners, it's important to understand that a higher Asset Turnover Ratio suggests better efficiency in utilizing assets to generate sales. However, this ratio should be used in conjunction with other financial ratios and analysis tools to understand a company's overall financial performance comprehensively. Comparing a company's Asset Turnover Ratio with industry benchmarks and competitors can provide valuable insights into its relative efficiency in generating sales from its assets.

Financial Ratios - Simple Summary

Liquidity ratios, such as the current and quick ratios, indicate a company's ability to meet short-term financial obligations.

Profitability ratios, like return on assets and equity, assess a company's profitability relative to its size.

Financial leverage ratios demonstrate how much a company relies on debt instead of shareholder investment to fund operations, which can increase both return on equity and business risk.

Asset turnover ratios, including inventory turnover and receivables turnover, measure how efficiently a company utilizes its assets. These ratios provide insights into a company's financial health and operational efficiency.

Financial Ratios - FAQs

1. What are Financial Ratios, and Why are They Important?

Financial ratios are quantitative measures to analyze a company's financial performance, operational efficiency, and overall health. They help investors, managers, and stakeholders assess a company's profitability, liquidity, solvency, and efficiency by comparing financial metrics. Understanding financial ratios can aid decision-making and benchmark against competitors or industry standards.

2. What are the Main Categories of Financial Ratios?

The main categories of financial ratios are liquidity ratios, profitability ratios, financial leverage ratios, asset turnover ratios, and market valuation ratios. Each category serves a specific purpose, evaluating a company's financial performance and health.

3. How Do I Calculate Financial Ratios?

To calculate financial ratios, you need to gather data from a company's financial statements, including the balance sheet, income statement, and cash flow statement. Once you have the necessary data, you can use specific formulas to calculate each ratio. For example, the current ratio is calculated by dividing current assets by current liabilities, while return on assets is calculated by dividing net income by average total assets.

4. How Do I Interpret Financial Ratios?

Interpreting financial ratios involves understanding their context and comparing them to historical data, industry benchmarks, and competitors' ratios. A single ratio alone might not provide sufficient information, so analyzing a set of ratios is essential to understand a company's financial health comprehensively. Ratios that deviate significantly from industry norms or historical trends may indicate areas that need further investigation or improvement.

5. Can Financial Ratios Predict a Company's Future Performance?

<u>While financial ratios can provide valuable insights into a company's financial health and operational efficiency, they are not foolproof predictors of future performance.</u> They are based on historical data and might not capture all the factors affecting a company's future growth and success. However, by using financial ratios in conjunction with other financial analysis tools, investors and managers can better understand a company's financial position and make more informed decisions.

Chapter 7: GAAP (Generally Accepted Accounting Principles)

GAAP, or Generally Accepted Accounting Principles, is a set of standardized accounting rules and guidelines that companies in the United States must follow when preparing their financial statements. These principles ensure consistency, transparency, and comparability in financial reporting, making it easier for investors, regulators, and other stakeholders to understand and analyze a company's financial performance.

GAAP is based on a few key principles:

1. **Consistency:** Companies should consistently apply the same accounting methods and policies from one accounting period to another, allowing for a more accurate comparison of financial data over time.
2. **Reliability:** Financial statements should provide a reliable and accurate representation of a company's financial position, performance, and cash flows.
3. **Relevance:** Financial information should be relevant to the users' decision-making process, meaning it should be timely, useful, and able to influence their decisions.
4. **Comparability:** Financial statements should be prepared in a way that allows users to compare the financial performance of different companies within the same industry easily.
5. **Materiality:** Information is considered material if its omission or misstatement could influence the users' decisions. Material information should be disclosed in the financial statements.

Who is Required to Follow GAAP?

GAAP, or Generally Accepted Accounting Principles, is a set of standardized accounting rules and guidelines for financial reporting in the United States. Companies that are required to follow GAAP include:

1. **Publicly-traded companies:** Companies that have issued stocks or bonds to the public and are listed on stock exchanges in the United States must follow GAAP when preparing their financial statements. This requirement ensures consistency and transparency in financial reporting, allowing investors to make informed decisions when evaluating and comparing investment options.
2. **Privately-held companies:** While privately-held companies are not legally required to follow GAAP, many choose to do so to maintain credibility with investors, lenders, and other stakeholders. Adhering to GAAP can make it easier for these companies to secure financing, attract investors, and facilitate business transactions.
3. **Non-profit organizations:** Non-profit organizations like charities and foundations are also encouraged to follow GAAP when preparing their financial statements. Doing so helps maintain transparency and accountability to donors, grant providers, and other stakeholders.
4. **Government entities:** Federal, state, and local government entities in the United States may follow GAAP or other specific accounting standards, such as the Governmental Accounting Standards Board (GASB) guidelines. Adhering to these principles helps ensure public funds are managed responsibly and transparently.

In summary, publicly-traded companies in the United States are legally required to follow GAAP, while privately-held companies, non-profit organizations, and government entities are encouraged to do so. Following GAAP helps maintain consistency, transparency, and comparability in financial reporting, making it easier for stakeholders to evaluate and compare the financial performance of different organizations.

The Matching Principle

The matching principle is a fundamental accounting principle that requires expenses to be recorded in the same accounting period as the revenue they helped to generate. This principle ensures that a company's financial statements accurately reflect its profitability and financial health.

Let's say that a company sells $5,000 in products in January but doesn't receive payment until February. The matching principle requires that the company records the revenue in January when it was earned, even though the payment wasn't received until the next month.

Now, let's say the company incurred $2,500 in expenses in January to produce and sell the products. The matching principle requires that the $2,500 in expenses be recorded in the same period as the $5,000 in revenue. This way, the company's financial statements accurately reflect the business's profitability during the period in question.

The matching principle's importance is ensuring that a company's financial statements accurately reflect its profitability and financial health. If a company were to record expenses in a different period from the corresponding revenue, it could distort its financial statements and misrepresent its financial performance. By matching expenses with revenue, the matching principle provides a more accurate picture of a company's profitability and helps management make informed financial decisions.

GAAP (Generally Accepted Accounting Principles) - Simple Summary

In summary, GAAP covers various aspects of accounting, such as revenue recognition, expense recognition, asset and liability measurement, and financial statement presentation. The Financial Accounting Standards Board (FASB) is responsible for developing and updating GAAP in the United States. Companies must adhere to GAAP when preparing their financial statements to provide a fair and accurate representation of their financial health, making it easier for investors and other stakeholders to make informed decisions.

Publicly traded companies in the United States are legally required to follow GAAP, while privately-held companies, non-profit organizations, and government entities are encouraged to do so. Following GAAP helps maintain consistency, transparency, and comparability in financial reporting, making it easier for stakeholders to evaluate and compare the financial performance of different organizations.

GAAP (Generally Accepted Accounting Principles) - FAQs
1. What is the Purpose of GAAP?

The purpose of GAAP (Generally Accepted Accounting Principles) is to ensure consistency, transparency, and comparability in financial reporting. By following these standardized rules and guidelines, companies can present their financial statements in a way that makes it easy for investors, regulators, and other stakeholders to understand and analyze their financial performance.

2. Who Sets and Regulates GAAP?

The Financial Accounting Standards Board (FASB), a private, non-profit organization, is responsible for establishing and updating GAAP in the United States. FASB works closely with the Securities and Exchange Commission (SEC), which has the legal authority to enforce GAAP for publicly-traded companies. The SEC ensures that companies adhere to GAAP when preparing their financial statements, helping to maintain credibility and transparency in financial reporting.

3. How Does GAAP Differ from IFRS?

GAAP is the set of accounting principles used in the United States, but the International Financial Reporting Standards (IFRS) is a set

<u>of global accounting standards.</u> IFRS was developed by the International Accounting Standards Board (IASB). While both GAAP and IFRS aim to provide consistency and transparency in financial reporting, there are differences in their rules, guidelines, and methods. Some of the key differences include revenue recognition, inventory valuation, and lease accounting. Many countries worldwide have adopted IFRS, making it essential for multinational companies to be familiar with both sets of accounting standards.

Chapter 8: Debits and Credits

Debits and credits are the fundamental building blocks of the double-entry bookkeeping system used in accounting. They represent the two sides of every financial transaction and help ensure that a company's accounts remain balanced.

Think back to the accounting equation: Assets = Liabilities + Owners' Equity.

In this system, every transaction affects at least two accounts: one is debited (increased), and another is credited (decreased). The basic rules for debits and credits are as follows:

- Asset accounts: When an asset increases, it is debited; when it decreases, it is credited.
- Liability accounts: When a liability increases, it is credited; when it decreases, it is debited.
- Equity accounts: When equity increases, it is credited; when it decreases, it is debited.
- Revenue accounts: When revenue increases, it is credited; when it decreases, it is debited.
- Expense accounts: When an expense increases, it is debited; when it decreases, it is credited.

Account Types Table - By Account Name, Type, Debit & Credit Determination

Accounting Made Simpler

Account	Type	Debit	Credit
ACCOUNTS PAYABLE	Liability	Decrease	Increase
ACCOUNTS RECEIVABLE	Asset	Increase	Decrease
ACCUMULATED DEPRECIATION	Contra Asset	Decrease	Increase
ADVERTISING EXPENSE	Expense	Increase	Decrease
ALLOWANCE FOR UNCOLLECTIBLE ACCOUNTS	Contra Asset	Decrease	Increase
AMORTIZATION EXPENSE	Expense	Increase	Decrease
AVAILABLE FOR SALE SECURITIES	Asset	Increase	Decrease
BONDS PAYABLE	Liability	Decrease	Increase
BUILDING	Asset	Increase	Decrease
CAPITAL STOCK	Equity	Decrease	Increase
CASH	Asset	Increase	Decrease
CASH OVER	Revenue	Decrease	Increase
CASH SHORT	Expense	Increase	Decrease
CHARITABLE CONTRIBUTIONS PAYABLE	Liability	Decrease	Increase
COMMON STOCK	Equity	Decrease	Increase
COST OF GOODS SOLD	Expense	Increase	Decrease

Accounting Made Simpler

Account	Type	Debit	Credit
CURRENCY EXCHANGE GAIN	Gain	Decrease	Increase
CURRENCY EXCHANGE LOSS	Loss	Increase	Decrease
DEPRECIATION EXPENSE	Expense	Increase	Decrease
DISCOUNT ON BONDS PAYABLE	Liability	Decrease	Increase
DISCOUNT ON NOTES PAYABLE	Contra Liability	Increase	Decrease
DIVIDEND INCOME	Revenue	Decrease	Increase
DIVIDENDS	Dividend	Increase	Decrease
DIVIDENDS PAYABLE	Liability	Decrease	Increase
DOMAIN NAME	Asset	Increase	Decrease
EMPLOYEE BENEFITS EXPENSE	Expense	Increase	Decrease
EQUIPMENT	Asset	Increase	Decrease
FEDERAL INCOME TAX PAYABLE	Liability	Decrease	Increase
FEDERAL UNEMPLOYMENT TAX PAYABLE	Liability	Decrease	Increase
FREIGHT-IN	Part of Calculation of Net Purchases	Increase	Decrease
FREIGHT-OUT	Expense	Increase	Decrease
FUEL EXPENSE	Expense	Increase	Decrease

Accounting Made Simpler

Account	Type	Debit	Credit
GAIN	Gain	Decrease	Increase
HEALTH/CHILD FLEX PAYABLE	Liability	Decrease	Increase
INCOME SUMMARY	Not a Financial Statement Account	Debited for Total Expenses	Credited for Total Revenue
INSURANCE EXPENSE	Expense	Increase	Decrease
INSURANCE PAYABLE	Liability	Decrease	Increase
INTEREST EXPENSE	Expense	Increase	Decrease
INTEREST INCOME	Revenue	Decrease	Increase
INTEREST PAYABLE	Liability	Decrease	Increase
INTEREST RECEIVABLE	Asset	Increase	Decrease
INVENTORY	Asset	Increase	Decrease
INVESTMENT IN BONDS	Asset	Increase	Decrease
INVESTMENT INCOME	Revenue	Decrease	Increase
INVESTMENTS	Asset	Increase	Decrease
LAND	Asset	Increase	Decrease
LOAN PAYABLE	Liability	Decrease	Increase
LOSS	Loss	Increase	Decrease
MEDICARE/MEDICAID PAYABLE	Liability	Decrease	Increase

Accounting Made Simpler

Account	Type	Debit	Credit
MISCELLANEOUS EXPENSE	Expense	Increase	Decrease
NOTES PAYABLE	Liability	Decrease	Increase
NOTES RECEIVABLE	Asset	Increase	Decrease
OBLIGATION UNDER CAPITAL LEASE	Liability	Decrease	Increase
PAID-IN CAPITAL IN EXCESS OF PAR– COMMON	Equity	Decrease	Increase
PAID-IN CAPITAL IN EXCESS OF PAR – PREFERRED	Equity	Decrease	Increase
PATENT	Asset	Increase	Decrease
PAYROLL TAX EXPENSE	Expense	Increase	Decrease
PETTY CASH	Asset	Increase	Decrease
POSTAGE EXPENSE	Expense	Increase	Decrease
PREMIUM ON BONDS PAYABLE	Liability Adjunct Account	Decrease	Increase
PREPAID INSURANCE	Asset	Increase	Decrease
PREPAID RENT	Asset	Increase	Decrease
PURCHASE DISCOUNTS	Reduces Calculation of Net Purchases	Decrease	Increase
PURCHASE DISCOUNTS LOST	Expense	Increase	Decrease

Accounting Made Simpler

Account	Type	Debit	Credit
PURCHASES	Part of Calculation of Net Purchases	Increase	Decrease
PURCHASE RETURNS	Reduces Calculation of Net Purchases	Decrease	Increase
RENT EXPENSE	Expense	Increase	Decrease
REPAIR EXPENSE	Expense	Increase	Decrease
RETAINED EARNINGS	Equity	Decrease	Increase
RETIREMENT CONTRIBUTION PAYABLE	Liability	Decrease	Increase
REVENUE	Revenue	Decrease	Increase
SALARIES EXPENSE	Expense	Increase	Decrease
SALARIES PAYABLE	Liability	Decrease	Increase
SALES	Revenue	Decrease	Increase
SALES DISCOUNTS	Contra Revenue	Increase	Decrease
SALES RETURNS	Contra Revenue	Increase	Decrease
SERVICE CHARGE	Expense	Increase	Decrease
SERVICE REVENUE	Revenue	Decrease	Increase
SOCIAL SECURITY PAYABLE	Liability	Decrease	Increase
STATE INCOME TAX PAYABLE	Liability	Decrease	Increase

Accounting Made Simpler

Account	Type	Debit	Credit
STATE UNEMPLOYMENT TAX PAYABLE	Liability	Decrease	Increase
SUPPLIES	Asset	Increase	Decrease
SUPPLIES EXPENSE	Expense	Increase	Decrease
TRADING SECURITIES	Asset	Increase	Decrease
TREASURY STOCK	Contra Equity	Increase	Decrease
UNCOLLECTIBLE ACCOUNTS EXPENSE	Expense	Increase	Decrease
UNEARNED REVENUE	Liability	Decrease	Increase
UNREALIZED GAIN	Gain	Decrease	Increase
UNREALIZED LOSS	Loss	Increase	Decrease
UNREALIZED GAIN – OTHER COMPREHENSIVE INCOME	Increase in Equity Via Other Comprehensive Income	Decrease	Increase
UNREALIZED LOSS – OTHER COMPREHENSIVE INCOME	Decrease in Equity Via Other Comprehensive Income	Increase	Decrease
UTILITIES EXPENSE	Expense	Increase	Decrease
WARRANTY EXPENSE	Expense	Increase	Decrease
WARRANTY LIABILITY	Liability	Decrease	Increase

Example:

Imagine a company purchases a piece of equipment for $5,000 in cash. In this transaction, two accounts are affected: the equipment account (an asset) and the cash account (an asset).

Since the equipment account is an asset account and the company's assets are increasing, it will be debited by $5,000. On the other hand, the cash account is also an asset account, but the company's cash is decreasing, so it will be credited by $5,000.

The journal entry for this transaction would look like this:

Debit: Equipment - $5,000

Credit: Cash - $5,000

By following the rules of debits and credits, the double-entry bookkeeping system helps ensure that a company's financial statements remain balanced and accurate.

Here are several examples of debit and credit accounting transactions, along with explanations for each:

Example A:

A company receives a $10,000 loan from a bank.

Explanation: In this transaction, the company's cash (an asset) increases by $10,000, so the cash account is debited. The loan (a liability) also increases by $10,000, so the loan account is credited.

Journal Entry:

Debit: Cash - $10,000

Credit: Loan - $10,000

Example B:

A company purchases inventory for $3,000 on credit.

Explanation: The company's inventory (an asset) increases by $3,000, so the inventory account is debited. Since the purchase is on credit, the accounts payable (a liability) also increase by $3,000, so the accounts payable account is credited.

Journal Entry:

Debit: Inventory - $3,000

Credit: Accounts Payable - $3,000

Example C:

A company sells goods for $5,000 cash.

Explanation: The company's cash (an asset) increases by $5,000, so the cash account is debited. The revenue from the sale (a revenue account) also increases by $5,000, so the revenue account is credited.

Journal Entry:

Debit: Cash - $5,000

Credit: Revenue - $5,000

Example D:

A company pays $1,500 in rent for its office space.

Explanation: The company's cash (an asset) decreases by $1,500, so the cash account is credited. The rent expense (an expense account) increases by $1,500, so the rent expense account is debited.

Journal Entry:

Debit: Rent Expense - $1,500

Credit: Cash - $1,500

Example E:

A company pays $2,000 to settle an accounts payable.

Explanation: The company's cash (an asset) decreases by $2,000, so the cash account is credited. The accounts payable (a liability) also decrease by $2,000, so the accounts payable account is debited.

Journal Entry:

Debit: Accounts Payable - $2,000

Credit: Cash - $2,000

These examples illustrate the basic rules for debits and credits in various types of accounting transactions. By understanding and applying these rules, beginners can develop a solid foundation in double-entry bookkeeping and maintain accurate financial records.

The General Ledger

The general ledger is a fundamental accounting tool that serves as a complete record of a company's financial transactions. It is organized into various accounts, each representing a specific category in the company's financial statements, such as assets, liabilities, equity, revenues, and expenses.

In a general ledger, transactions are recorded using the double-entry bookkeeping system, which means that for every transaction, there are at least two corresponding entries: a debit and a credit. These entries are made to different accounts in the general ledger to ensure that the accounting equation (Assets = Liabilities + Equity) remains balanced.

Each account in the general ledger has a unique account number and is divided into two columns: debits on the left and credits on the right. The difference between the total debits and credits for an account is called the account balance. At the end of a reporting period, the balances of all accounts in the general ledger are used to create the company's financial statements, such as the balance sheet and income statement.

In summary, the general ledger is a crucial accounting tool that records a company's financial transactions using the double-entry bookkeeping system. It maintains a complete and organized record of a company's financial activities, essential for accurate financial reporting and decision-making.

The Trial Balance

A trial balance is a financial statement that lists the balances of all accounts in the general ledger at a specific time, usually at the end of a reporting period, such as a month or a year. A trial balance aims to ensure that the total debits equal the total credits across all accounts and to detect any errors that may have occurred in the accounting process.

A trial balance consists of a two-column table, with each account in the left column and the corresponding balance in the right column. The debit balances are listed as positive numbers, while the credit balances are listed as negative numbers. The sum of all the debit balances should equal the sum of all the credit balances. If the two sides do not balance, it indicates an error in the accounting records that must be corrected.

The trial balance is an important step in the accounting process, as it helps ensure the accuracy of the financial statements that are prepared based on the general ledger balances. It is also useful for identifying errors and inconsistencies in the accounting records, such as double or missing entries.

In summary, a trial balance is a financial statement that lists the balances of all accounts in the general ledger and ensures that the total debits equal the total credits. It is an important tool for ensuring the accuracy of financial statements and identifying errors in accounting records.

T-Accounts

T-accounts are a simple and visual tool used in accounting to represent individual accounts within a company's general ledger. They are called T-accounts because they are shaped like the letter "T," with a horizontal line at the top and a vertical line down the middle, dividing the account into two columns.

The left column of a T-account is for recording debit entries, while the right column is for recording credit entries. T-accounts follow the same rules of debits and credits as the double-entry bookkeeping system used in general ledgers. In this system, every financial transaction results in at least one debit and credit entry, ensuring that the accounting equation (Assets = Liabilities + Equity) remains balanced.

T-accounts are often used as a learning tool or for informal record-keeping to help visualize the impact of transactions on specific accounts. They can also help identify errors and understand the flow of transactions within the accounting system.

To use a T-account, write the account name at the top of the "T." Then, record the debits and credits for each transaction that impacts the account in the respective columns. At the end of a reporting period or when needed, calculate the account balance by subtracting the total credits from the total debits.

In summary, T-accounts are a simple and visual representation of individual accounts within a general ledger, used to track debits and credits and to help understand the impact of transactions on specific accounts. They are particularly useful for beginners learning the principles of double-entry bookkeeping and the rules of debits and credits.

Let's take a simple example to illustrate how T-accounts work. Suppose a small business has the following transactions:

The owner invests $5,000 in the business (cash contribution).

The business purchases equipment worth $2,000 in cash.

We will create T-accounts for the Cash and Equipment accounts to record these transactions.

Cash Account (Asset):

  Debits | Credits

$5,000 | $2,000

Equipment Account (Asset):

  Debits | Credits

$2,000 | $0

Here's the explanation for each transaction:

The owner invests $5,000 in the business. This increases the company's cash (an asset), so we record a debit of $5,000 in the Cash account.

The business purchases equipment worth $2,000 in cash. This increases the company's equipment (an asset), so we record a debit of $2,000 in the Equipment account. Since the purchase was made with cash, the company's cash (an asset) decreased, so we record a credit of $2,000 in the Cash account.

After recording these transactions, we can determine the balance of each account:

Cash Account: Debits ($5,000) - Credits ($2,000) = $3,000

Equipment Account: Debits ($2,000) - Credits ($0) = $2,000

This example demonstrates how T-accounts can represent individual accounts within a general ledger, track debits and credits, and understand the impact of transactions on specific accounts.

Debits and Credits - Simple Summary

In accounting, every transaction must be recorded through a **journal entry** consisting of a debit and a credit.

Debits are used to increase asset accounts and decrease equity and liability accounts, while **credits** have the opposite effect of decreasing asset accounts and increasing equity and liability accounts.

Additionally, **expense accounts** are increased by debits, while credits increase **revenue accounts**.

Debits and Credits - FAQs
1. What is the Difference Between Debit and Credit?

Debit and credit are two terms used in accounting to describe the movement of funds in a financial transaction. <u>A debit is an entry that increases an asset account or decreases a liability or equity account, but a credit is an entry that increases a liability or equity account or decreases an asset account.</u>

2. Why are Debit and Credit Used in Accounting?

Debit and credit are used in accounting to ensure that every transaction is recorded accurately and consistently. <u>By using a standardized system of debits and credits, accountants can easily keep track of the financial status of a business and make sure that the books balance.</u>

3. How Do I Know When to Use a Debit or Credit?

The rule of thumb in accounting is "Debits on the left, credits on the right." <u>This means that one account will be debited for every transaction, and one account will be credited.</u> The account to be debited or credited depends on the type of transaction being recorded. For example, when a company makes a sale, the cash account will be debited (increased), and the revenue account will be credited (increased). Understanding which accounts to debit or credit comes with practice and familiarity with accounting principles.

Chapter 9: Cash vs. Accrual

Cash and accrual accounting are two methods to track a business's financial transactions. The primary difference between the two methods is the timing of when revenue and expenses are recognized.

Cash accounting is a method where revenue and expenses are recorded when cash is received or paid out. Small businesses or individuals often use this method because it is simple to use and understand. For example, if a small business sells a product for $1,000 and the customer pays in cash, the business records the revenue of $1,000 when the cash is received.

Accrual accounting, on the other hand, is a method where revenue and expenses are recognized when earned or incurred, regardless of when the money is received or paid. Larger businesses or organizations often use this method because it provides a more accurate picture of the company's financial performance over time. For example, if a company provides a service for a customer in January but does not receive payment until February, the company would still recognize the revenue in January, when the service was provided.

Here is a summary of the differences between cash and accrual accounting:

- **Cash accounting:** Revenue and expenses are recorded when cash is received or paid out.

- **Accrual accounting:** Revenue and expenses are recognized when earned or incurred, regardless of when the money is received or paid.

Examples:

Cash accounting: A small business owner sells a product for $500 in December 2021 but receives payment in January 2022. The revenue will be recorded in January 2022, when the cash is received.

Accrual accounting: A large company provides consulting services in December 2021 but does not receive payment until January 2022. The revenue will be recorded in December 2021, when the services were provided, even though the cash was not received until January 2022.

How Cash vs. Accrual Accounting Can Make a Business Profitable

Cash and accrual accounting can impact a business's profitability in different ways. Cash accounting may make a business appear more profitable in the short term since revenue and expenses are only recorded when cash is exchanged. This means that the business can delay recording expenses until later, making it seem like it has more cash on hand than it does. However, this can also make it more difficult to plan for the future, as the business may not have a clear picture of its financial performance.

On the other hand, accrual accounting can make a business appear less profitable in the short term since it recognizes revenue and expenses when earned or incurred, regardless of when the money is received or paid. This means that a business may have to record expenses before it has received payment for its products or services, which can impact its cash flow. However, accrual accounting provides a more accurate picture of a business's financial performance over time, which can help it make better decisions about future investments.

Example:

Here is an example to illustrate the difference between cash and accrual accounting:

A small business sells $10,000 worth of products in December 2021. Under cash accounting, the business would only recognize this revenue in January 2022 if it receives payment from the customer that month. However, under accrual accounting, the business would recognize this revenue in December 2021, when the products were sold, regardless of whether or not payment was received in that month.

If the business used cash accounting, it would have less revenue recorded in December 2021, which could make it seem less profitable. However, if it used accrual accounting, it would have more revenue recorded in December 2021, which could make it seem more profitable. Ultimately, cash and accrual accounting depends on a business's specific needs and circumstances. It is important to consult a financial professional to determine the best method.

Cash vs. Accrual - Simple Summary

Cash and accrual accounting are two methods to track a business's financial transactions. The primary difference between the two methods is the timing of when revenue and expenses are recognized. Cash accounting records revenue and expenses when cash is received or paid out. In contrast, accrual accounting records revenue and expenses when earned or incurred, regardless of when the money is received or paid.

The importance of cash vs. accrual accounting lies in its impact on a business's financial performance and decision-making. Cash accounting may make a business appear more profitable in the short term, but it can also make it more difficult to plan for the future.

On the other hand, accrual accounting provides a more accurate picture of a business's financial performance over time, which can help it make better decisions about future investments. Ultimately, cash and accrual accounting depends on a business's specific needs and circumstances.

Cash vs. Accrual - FAQs

1. What is the Main Difference Between Cash and Accrual Accounting?

The main difference between cash and accrual accounting is the timing of when revenue and expenses are recognized. Cash accounting records revenue and expenses when cash is received or paid out. In contrast, accrual accounting records revenue and expenses when earned or incurred, regardless of when the money is received or paid.

2. Which Method is Better for my Business, Cash or Accrual Accounting?

Cash and accrual accounting depends on a business's specific needs and circumstances. Cash accounting may be simpler for small businesses with fewer transactions. In contrast, accrual accounting provides a more accurate picture of a business's financial performance over time, which can help it make better decisions about future investments. It is important to consult with a financial professional to determine which method is best for your business.

3. Is One Method More Accurate Than the Other?

Both cash and accrual accounting are accurate methods of tracking a business's financial transactions. The choice between the two methods depends on a business's specific needs and circumstances.

4. Can I Switch From Cash to Accrual Accounting or Vice Versa?

Yes, a business can switch from cash to accrual accounting or vice versa. However, it is important to consult with a financial professional before making the switch, as it can impact when revenue and expenses are recognized.

5. How Does Cash vs. Accrual Accounting Impact my Taxes?

The method of accounting a business uses can impact its taxes. <u>The IRS requires businesses with more than $25 million in average annual gross receipts for the preceding three years to use the accrual method of accounting. Smaller businesses may be able to use either cash or accrual accounting, depending on their specific circumstances.</u> It is important to consult with a financial professional to determine which method is best for your business's tax situation.

Chapter 10: Fixed Asset Depreciation

Fixed asset depreciation spreads the cost of a long-term asset over its useful life. It is a way of allocating the asset's cost over the period in which it is expected to benefit the company. The importance of fixed asset depreciation lies in the fact that it helps to match the cost of the asset with the revenue it generates.

For example, a company purchases a machine for $100,000 with a useful life of 10 years. Instead of recording the entire cost of the machine in the year it was purchased, the company can use depreciation to allocate the cost over the 10-year useful life of the machine. If the company uses the straight-line method of depreciation, it would divide the cost of the machine by 10 to get a depreciation expense of $10,000 per year.

In this case, the company's income statement would show a $10,000 expense for depreciation each year, which would reduce the company's taxable income. At the same time, the company's balance sheet would show the machine's cost of $100,000 reduced by $10,000 each year, reflecting the decrease in the machine's value over time.

The importance of fixed asset depreciation lies in its providing a more accurate representation of a company's financial performance by spreading the asset's cost over its useful life. Without depreciation, a company's income statement would show a significant expense in the year the asset was purchased, even though the benefits of the asset would be realized over several years. Using depreciation, a company can more accurately reflect the asset's cost over time and accurately represent its financial performance.

There are several fixed asset depreciation methods, and each method calculates depreciation slightly differently.

Here are three commonly used methods:

1. **Straight-Line Method:** This is the simplest and most commonly used depreciation method. It calculates depreciation by dividing the asset's cost by its useful life. For example, if a company buys a machine for $100,000 with a useful life of 10 years, it would depreciate the machine by $10,000 per year for 10 years.
2. **Double-Declining Balance Method:** This method calculates depreciation at an accelerated rate by applying a constant percentage to the asset's book value. The book value is the cost of the asset minus accumulated depreciation. For example, if a company buys a machine for $100,000 with a useful life of 10 years, it would calculate depreciation at 20% per year (double the straight-line rate of 10%). The machine's book value in the first year is $100,000, so the depreciation expense would be $20,000 (20% of $100,000). In the second year, the book value would be $80,000 ($100,000 - $20,000), and the depreciation expense would be $16,000 (20% of $80,000). The depreciation expense decreases each year as the book value of the asset declines.
3. **Units-of-Production Method:** This method calculates depreciation based on the asset's usage or production level. It divides the asset's cost by the number of units it is expected to produce or the number of hours it is expected to operate. For example, if a company buys a machine for $100,000 that is expected to produce 1 million units over its useful life of 5 years, it would depreciate the machine by $0.10 per unit ($100,000 / 1,000,000 units). If the machine produces 200,000 units in the first year, the

depreciation expense would be $20,000 (200,000 units x $0.10 per unit).

These methods are important for beginners to understand because they help companies accurately report the decline in value of their long-term assets over time. Choosing the appropriate depreciation method can also affect a company's profitability and tax liability.

Accumulated Depreciation

Accumulated Depreciation is a contra-asset account representing the total depreciation expense taken on a fixed asset since the time of acquisition. It is a running total of all the depreciation charges recorded on a fixed asset.

For example, a company purchases a piece of machinery for $50,000 with a useful life of 10 years and no salvage value. Using the straight-line depreciation method, the annual depreciation expense is $5,000 ($50,000/10 years). At the end of the first year, the accumulated depreciation account will have a balance of $5,000 ($5,000 in depreciation expense for the year). At the end of the second year, the accumulated depreciation account will have a balance of $10,000 ($5,000 in depreciation expense for the year, plus the $5,000 balance from the previous year), and so on.

The accumulated depreciation account is important because it helps accurately reflect a fixed asset's value on a company's balance sheet. The balance sheet reports the original cost of the asset, less accumulated depreciation, which results in the asset's net book value. The net book value estimates how much the asset is worth at a given time, considering its age and the amount of wear and tear it has experienced.

Accumulated depreciation is also important because it allows a company to track the remaining useful life of a fixed asset. By subtracting the accumulated depreciation from the asset's original cost, a company can determine the net book value, which can be compared to the asset's current market value. This information is useful in determining whether to sell or dispose of an asset or to continue using it.

Salvage Value

Salvage value is the estimated value a fixed asset will have at the end of its useful life after fully depreciating. When calculating depreciation, the salvage value is subtracted from the asset's original cost, and the remaining amount is divided by the number of years of its useful life.

For example, suppose a company purchases a machine for $100,000, which has a useful life of 5 years and an estimated salvage value of $10,000. Using the straight-line method, the annual depreciation expense would be $18,000 ($100,000 - $10,000 divided by 5 years). At the end of the machine's useful life, the company expects to sell the machine for $10,000, the estimated salvage value.

Salvage value is important because it affects the amount of depreciation that is recorded each year. A higher salvage value will result in lower depreciation expenses, while a lower salvage value will result in higher depreciation expenses. The salvage value also affects the gain or loss recognized when an asset is sold or disposed of at the end of its useful life. If the sale price exceeds the salvage value, a gain will be recognized, and a loss will be recognized if it is lower.

Therefore, businesses need to estimate the salvage value accurately to ensure that they properly record the decline in value of their fixed assets over time and make informed decisions about when to retire or sell an asset.

Gain or Loss on Sale

Gain or loss on the sale of an asset is the difference between the sales price and the carrying amount of a fixed asset that has been sold or disposed of at the end of its useful life. The carrying amount of an asset is its original cost minus the total accumulated depreciation.

For example, suppose a company sells a machine with an original cost of $100,000, which had been fully depreciated over its useful life of 5 years. The company had estimated a salvage value of $10,000 for the machine. At the end of its useful life, the machine was sold for $12,000.

The carrying amount of the machine would be $0 ($100,000 - $18,000 per year of depreciation x 5 years). The sales price of $12,000 is greater than the estimated salvage value of $10,000, resulting in a gain of $2,000 ($12,000 - $10,000).

A loss would be recognized instead of a gain if the sales price was less than the estimated salvage value. For example, if the machine were sold for $8,000 instead of $12,000, a loss of $2,000 would be recognized ($8,000 - $10,000).

The gain or loss on the sale of an asset is important because it affects the financial statements and the calculation of taxable income. Gains on sales increase income and taxable income, while losses decrease income and taxable income. Therefore, it is important for businesses to accurately record and report any gains or losses on the sale or disposal of fixed assets.

Capitalize vs. Expense a Fixed Asset

When a business purchases a fixed asset, it has to decide whether to capitalize or expense the asset's cost—capitalizing means that the asset's cost is added to the company's balance sheet as an asset and is then gradually depreciated over the asset's useful life. Expensing means the asset's cost is immediately recorded as an expense in the income statement.

The decision to capitalize or expense a fixed asset depends on whether the asset meets certain criteria. **According to Generally Accepted Accounting Principles (GAAP), an asset should be capitalized if it meets these three criteria**:

1. The asset has a useful life of more than one year.
2. The asset is used in the company's operations to generate revenue.
3. The asset's cost is significant (usually a minimum dollar amount).

For example, a company purchases a new delivery truck for $50,000. The truck is expected to have a useful life of 5 years and will be used to make deliveries to customers, generating revenue for the company. The cost of the truck is considered significant, so it meets all three criteria for capitalization. The company would capitalize on the cost of the truck and then depreciate it over its useful life.

On the other hand, if the company had purchased office supplies for $50, it would be expensed immediately since the supplies do not have a useful life of more than one year, and they are not used to generate revenue for the company.

It is important to properly classify fixed assets as capitalized or expensed since it can have a significant impact on the company's financial statements and profitability. By capitalizing an asset, the company can spread the asset's cost over its useful life, reducing the impact on the income statement in a single period.

Fixed Asset Depreciation - Simple Summary

Fixed Asset Depreciation is a process that spreads the cost of a fixed asset over its useful life to reflect its declining value over time accurately. This process helps companies to account for their assets and expenses in a way that reflects the economic reality of their operations.

There are various methods for calculating depreciation, including straight-line, declining balance, and sum-of-the-years-digits, each with its own advantages and disadvantages. The choice of method will depend on various factors, such as the type of asset, its useful life, and the company's accounting policies.

Salvage value is an important consideration in depreciation because it represents the expected value of the asset at the end of its useful life and can impact the amount of depreciation expense recognized each period. Gain or loss on sale is another important concept, which represents the difference between the asset's net book value and the sale price and must be recorded in the financial statements.

Accumulated depreciation is a contra-asset account representing the total depreciation expense taken on a fixed asset since the acquisition. It is important because it helps accurately reflect the value of a fixed asset on a company's balance sheet. It also allows a company to track the remaining useful life of a fixed asset.

Overall, the process of fixed asset depreciation is an important component of accounting, helping to ensure that companies accurately reflect the value of their assets and expenses in their financial statements.

Fixed Asset Depreciation - FAQs

1. What is Fixed Asset Depreciation?

Fixed asset depreciation is the process of spreading the cost of a fixed asset over its useful life to reflect its declining value over time accurately.

2. Why is Fixed Asset Depreciation Important?

Fixed asset depreciation is important because it helps companies to account for their assets and expenses in a way that reflects the economic reality of their operations. It also ensures that fixed asset value is accurately reflected on a company's balance sheet.

3. What are the Different Methods of Fixed Asset Depreciation?

There are various methods for calculating depreciation, including straight-line, declining balance, and sum-of-the-years-digits, each with advantages and disadvantages. The choice of method will depend on various factors, such as the type of asset, its useful life, and the company's accounting policies.

4. What is Salvage Value, and How Does it Impact Depreciation?

Salvage value is the expected value of a fixed asset at the end of its useful life and can impact the depreciation expense recognized each period. When calculating depreciation, it is important to consider because it represents the asset's residual value.

5. What is Accumulated Depreciation?

Accumulated depreciation is a contra-asset account representing the total depreciation expense taken on a fixed asset since the acquisition. It is important because it helps accurately reflect a fixed asset's value on a company's balance sheet and allows a company to track its remaining useful life.

Chapter 11: Intangible Asset Amortization

Intangible asset amortization systematically expenses an intangible asset's cost over its useful life. This is done similarly to fixed asset depreciation, but intangible assets such as patents, copyrights, and trademarks are not physical.

For example, suppose a company spends $100,000 to obtain a patent with a useful life of 10 years. The company would divide the cost of the patent by its useful life to determine the annual amortization expense, which in this case would be $10,000 per year. The amortization expense is then recognized on the income statement each year over the patent's useful life.

Another example is a company that spends $500,000 to develop a proprietary software program. The company may choose to amortize the cost of the software over its estimated useful life of 5 years. The annual amortization expense would be $100,000 per year, calculated by dividing the total cost of the software by its useful life.

Intangible asset amortization is important because it helps to match the cost of acquiring or creating an intangible asset with the periods in which the asset generates revenue. This allows a company to accurately reflect the value of its intangible assets on the balance sheet and in financial statements, providing a more complete picture of the company's financial performance.

What Intangible Assets Can Be Amortized?

Under GAAP, intangible assets that can be amortized include:

1. **Patents:** Legal protection for an invention or process that provides exclusive rights to the patent holder for a specified period of time.
2. **Trademarks:** A symbol, word, or phrase used to identify and distinguish a company's products or services from its competitors.
3. **Copyrights:** Legal protection for original works of authorship, including books, music, and software.
4. **Franchise agreements:** A contractual agreement that allows a company to use another company's trademark, products, or business methods in exchange for a fee.
5. **Licenses:** Legal agreements that allow a company to use another company's products or services in exchange for a fee.
6. **Customer lists:** A collection of information about a company's customers used for marketing or other business purposes.
7. **Non-compete agreements:** Legal agreements that prohibit an employee or former owner from competing with the company for a specified period of time.

For example, suppose a company purchases a patent for $50,000 with a useful life of 10 years. The company would amortize the cost of the patent over its useful life, recognizing $5,000 of amortization expense each year on the income statement.

Another example is a company that purchases a trademark for $100,000 that has a useful life of 20 years. The company would amortize the cost of the trademark over its useful life, recognizing $5,000 of amortization expense each year on the income statement.

Intangible asset amortization is important because it allows a company to spread the cost of an intangible asset over its useful life rather than recognizing the entire cost in a single period. This helps to accurately reflect the value of intangible assets on the balance sheet and financial statements, providing a more complete picture of the company's financial performance.

Intangible Asset Amortization - Simple Summary

Intangible asset amortization refers to spreading out the cost of intangible assets over their useful lives rather than recognizing the entire cost in a single period. Intangible assets that can be amortized include patents, trademarks, copyrights, franchise agreements, licenses, customer lists, and non-compete agreements.

The amortization process allows a company to accurately reflect the value of intangible assets on the balance sheet and in financial statements, providing a more complete picture of the company's financial performance. By amortizing intangible assets, a company can avoid a large one-time expense and instead recognize a smaller expense over the asset's useful life.

Intangible Asset Amortization - FAQs

1. What is an Intangible Asset?

An intangible asset is an asset that lacks physical substance but has value, such as patents, trademarks, copyrights, and goodwill.

2. What is Intangible Asset Amortization?

Intangible asset amortization refers to the process of spreading out the cost of intangible assets over their useful lives rather than recognizing the entire cost in a single period.

3. How is the Useful Life of an Intangible Asset Determined?

The useful life of an intangible asset is determined based on how long the asset is expected to provide benefits to the company. This can be estimated based on legal or contractual terms, expected changes in the marketplace, and the expected life of any associated products or services.

4. How is the Amortization Expense Calculated?

The amortization expense is calculated by dividing the intangible asset's cost by its useful life. For example, if a patent costs $100,000 and has a useful life of 10 years, the annual amortization expense would be $10,000.

5. What is the Impact of Intangible Asset Amortization on Financial Statements?

Intangible asset amortization directly impacts the income statement, which is recorded as an expense, and the balance sheet, where the accumulated amortization is deducted from the asset's original cost to determine its net book value. This process provides a more accurate reflection of the asset's value over time and its impact on the company's financial performance.

Chapter 12: Inventory & Cost of Goods Sold (COGS)

Inventory refers to a company's goods and materials for resale or production. Cost of Goods Sold (COGS) refers to the direct cost of producing the goods sold by a company.

Inventory is an important aspect of a company's financial health because it represents a significant investment of resources. A company must carefully manage its inventory levels to ensure that it has enough stock to meet customer demand but not so much that it ties up too much capital or leads to losses due to spoilage, obsolescence, or theft.

COGS is also an important financial metric because it directly impacts a company's gross profit. Gross profit is calculated by subtracting COGS from revenue and represents the amount of money a company has left over after accounting for the direct costs of producing its goods. A higher gross profit margin indicates that a company can sell its products for a higher price than it costs to produce them, which is generally seen as a positive indicator of financial health.

For example, let's say a company produces and sells widgets. The company has $100,000 worth of widgets in inventory at the beginning of the year and purchases an additional $50,000 worth of widgets throughout the year. By the end of the year, the company has sold $120,000 worth of widgets. The company must determine the cost of the sold widgets to calculate COGS. Let's say that the cost of the widgets sold was $60,000. The company's gross profit for the year would be $60,000 ($120,000 revenue - $60,000 COGS), which represents the amount of money the company has left over to cover its other expenses and generate a profit.

Perpetual Inventory Method

The perpetual inventory method is a system businesses use to track inventory balances continuously, allowing them to maintain a more accurate record of their inventory levels. Under this method, each time a product is sold, the cost of the product is immediately transferred from the inventory account to the cost of goods sold account.

For example, let's say that a retail store uses the perpetual inventory method and sells a shirt for $20 that had been purchased for $10. As soon as the sale is made, the cost of the shirt is recorded in the cost of goods sold account, reducing the inventory balance by $10.

The perpetual inventory method is important because it allows businesses to keep a more accurate record of their inventory levels, reducing the likelihood of overstocking or running out of stock. It also helps businesses track the cost of goods sold, essential for determining profitability and making informed business decisions.

Periodic Inventory Method

The periodic inventory method is a system businesses use to track inventory balances periodically, usually at the end of each accounting period. Under this method, the cost of goods sold is determined by subtracting the ending inventory balance from the beginning inventory balance and then adding the cost of purchases made during the period.

For example, let's say that a retailer uses the periodic inventory method and has a beginning inventory balance of $10,000, makes purchases totaling $5,000 during the accounting period, and has an ending inventory balance of $8,000. The cost of goods sold would be calculated as follows:

Beginning inventory balance: $10,000

Purchases: $5,000

Total available inventory: $15,000

Ending inventory balance: $8,000

Cost of goods sold: $7,000 ($15,000 - $8,000)

The periodic inventory method is important because it allows businesses to determine the cost of goods sold at the end of each accounting period, which is necessary for calculating profitability and making informed business decisions. However, because it relies on periodic physical inventory counts, it can be more time-consuming and prone to errors than the perpetual inventory method.

How to Calculate COGS under the Perpetual and Periodic Method of Inventory

Under the perpetual inventory method, the cost of goods sold (CoGS) is calculated each time a sale is made by subtracting the cost of the sold item from the inventory account. The formula for calculating CoGS under the perpetual inventory method is:

Beginning inventory + Purchases - Ending inventory = Cost of goods sold

Examples:

Let's say a company has a beginning inventory of $50,000, makes purchases worth $100,000 during the period, and has an ending inventory of $40,000. The CoGS for the period would be:

$50,000 + $100,000 - $40,000 = $110,000

Under the periodic inventory method, the CoGS is calculated at the end of the period by subtracting the ending inventory from the sum of the beginning inventory and purchases. The formula for calculating CoGS under the periodic inventory method is:

Beginning inventory + Purchases - Ending inventory = Cost of goods sold

For example, let's say a company has a beginning inventory of $50,000, makes purchases worth $100,000 during the period, and has an ending inventory of $40,000. The CoGS for the period would be:

($50,000 + $100,000) - $40,000 = $110,000

The difference between the two methods is the frequency of inventory count. The perpetual method updates inventory accounts each time a sale is made, while the periodic method updates the accounts only at the end of the period. Both methods are acceptable under generally accepted accounting principles (GAAP). Still, the perpetual method provides more up-to-date inventory information, while the periodic method is simpler and less costly.

FIFO and Average Cost Methodologies of Inventory Accounting

FIFO and average cost methodologies are two ways to account for inventory costs in a business. FIFO stands for First-In, First-Out, meaning that the oldest inventory items are sold first. On the other hand, average cost takes the total cost of inventory and divides it by the total number of items to find an average cost per unit.

Example:

Let's say a business purchases 100 units of a product at $5 per unit and then purchases an additional 100 units at $6 per unit. The business sells 120 units of the product in a period. Under the FIFO method, the first 100 units sold would be assigned a cost of $5 per unit, and the remaining 20 units sold would be assigned a cost of

$6 per unit. The cost of goods sold would be calculated as (100 x $5) + (20 x $6) = $580.

Under the average cost method, the total cost of the 200 units of inventory would be divided by the total number of units to find an average cost per unit of $5.50. The cost of goods sold would be calculated as 120 units x $5.50 per unit = $660.

Both methods have their advantages and disadvantages. FIFO can result in a more accurate reflection of the current inventory cost, but it can also lead to older, less desirable inventory being held in stock. The average cost method is simpler to calculate and can smooth out fluctuations in inventory costs, but it may not accurately reflect the current inventory cost.

Inventory & Cost of Goods Sold (COGS) - Simple Summary

Inventory is a company's goods and materials for sale to customers. The cost of goods sold (COGS) is the direct cost of producing and delivering those goods and materials to customers.

There are two primary methods for inventory accounting: perpetual and periodic. In the perpetual method, the inventory account is continuously updated as goods are bought and sold, allowing for real-time inventory tracking. In the periodic method, the inventory account is only updated at the end of the accounting period, based on a physical count of inventory on hand.

To calculate COGS, it is necessary to determine the cost of goods sold during a specific accounting period. This can be done using either the FIFO (first-in, first-out) or average cost methods. FIFO assumes that the oldest inventory is sold first, while the average cost method takes the average cost of all inventory sold during the period.

It is essential to track inventory accurately and for COGS to maintain accurate financial statements and make informed business decisions. Inventory management can also impact a company's profitability, as holding too much inventory can tie up cash flow, while insufficient inventory can result in lost sales.

Inventory & Cost of Goods Sold (COGS) - FAQs

1. What is the Cost of Goods Sold (COGS)?

Cost of Goods Sold (COGS) represents the direct cost of producing goods sold by a company during a given period. It includes the cost of raw materials, direct labor, and overhead expenses incurred to produce goods.

2. How is COGS Calculated?

COGS can be calculated using either the periodic or perpetual inventory methods. Under the periodic inventory method, COGS is calculated by subtracting the ending inventory from the sum of the beginning inventory and purchases made during the period. Under the perpetual inventory method, COGS is calculated continuously throughout the accounting period based on the cost of each unit sold.

3. What is the Difference Between FIFO and Average Cost Methods of Inventory Accounting?

FIFO (First-In, First-Out) and average cost are two methods of inventory accounting used to determine the cost of goods sold and the value of ending inventory. FIFO assumes that the first items purchased are the first items sold, while average cost assumes that the cost of each unit is the average cost of all units purchased.

4. What is the Significance of Inventory Management?

Inventory management is essential for any business that sells physical products. Effective inventory management can help businesses minimize costs associated with holding inventory while ensuring they have enough stock to meet customer demand.

5. How Does the Inventory Turnover Ratio Relate to COGS?

The inventory turnover ratio is a financial ratio that measures how many times a company's inventory has been sold and replaced over a given period. It is calculated by dividing the cost of goods sold by the average inventory. <u>A high inventory turnover indicates that a company is selling its products quickly and efficiently, while a low ratio may indicate sales or inventory management issues.</u>

Conclusion & Wrap-Up

As we have learned in this brief book, accounting aims to provide information about a company's finances to internal and external users through financial statements.

The information is compiled from the general ledger, a collection of all the business's journal entries. Journal entries, consisting of debits and credits, are the building blocks upon which financial decisions are made in the business world.

These journal entries are based on the accounting equation and double-entry accounting system, with guidelines provided by GAAP to ensure consistency in financial reporting. Making meaningful comparisons between companies' financial statements would be impossible without GAAP.

Helpful Online Resources
To explore more accounting content, check out the following websites:

https://www.cfoconsultants.net/

https://www.benjaminwann.com/

Glossary

Accrual Accounting: An accounting method that records revenues and expenses when they are earned or incurred, regardless of when the cash is received or paid.

Accumulated Depreciation: The total amount of depreciation expense that has been recorded for an asset over its useful life.

Asset Accounts: Accounts that represent the resources owned by a business, such as cash, inventory, equipment, and buildings.

Asset Turnover Ratios: Ratios that measure how efficiently a company is utilizing its assets to generate sales.

Assets: Resources owned by a business that have economic value and can be used to generate future benefits.

Average Cost: A method of valuing inventory, where the cost of each unit is determined by dividing the total cost of goods available for sale by the total number of units available for sale.

Balance Sheet: A financial statement that provides a snapshot of a company's financial position by showing its assets, liabilities, and equity at a specific point in time.

Cash Accounting: An accounting method that records revenues and expenses when cash is received or paid.

Cash Flow Statement: A financial statement that shows the inflows and outflows of cash from operating, investing, and financing activities during a specific period of time.

Cost of Goods Sold (COGS): The direct costs associated with producing or purchasing the goods that a company sells.

Credits: Entries made on the right side of a ledger account, representing a decrease in assets or an increase in liabilities or equity.

Debits: Entries made on the left side of a ledger account, representing an increase in assets or a decrease in liabilities or equity.

Dividends: Distributions of profits to shareholders of a corporation.

Double-Declining Balance Method: A method of calculating depreciation that accelerates the recognition of depreciation expense in the early years of an asset's useful life.

Equity: The residual interest in the assets of a company after deducting liabilities.

Equity Accounts: Accounts that represent the owner's or shareholders' equity in a business, such as retained earnings and common stock.

Expense Accounts: Accounts that represent the costs incurred by a business in its normal operations, such as salaries, utilities, and advertising expenses.

First-In, First-Out (FIFO): A method of valuing inventory, where the cost of each unit is based on the assumption that the first units purchased or produced are the first ones sold.

Financial Leverage Ratios: Ratios that measure the extent to which a company uses debt financing to support its operations and generate returns for shareholders.

Financial Ratios: Ratios that provide insight into a company's financial performance and position by comparing different financial variables.

Financing Activities: Activities related to obtaining or repaying funds from external sources, such as issuing or repurchasing stock, issuing or retiring debt, or paying dividends.

Fixed Asset Depreciation: The systematic allocation of the cost of a fixed asset over its useful life to reflect its gradual wear and tear or obsolescence.

Gain on Sale: The amount by which the proceeds from the sale of an asset exceed its carrying value.

General Ledger: A master accounting record that contains all the accounts used by a company.

Generally Accepted Accounting Principles (GAAPs): Standard accounting rules and guidelines that govern how financial statements are prepared and presented.

Gross Profit: The difference between net sales revenue and the cost of goods sold.

Income Statement: A financial statement that summarizes a company's revenues, expenses, gains, and losses over a specific period of time, resulting in the calculation of net income or net loss.

Intangible Asset Amortization: The systematic allocation of the cost of an intangible asset over its useful life, such as patents or trademarks.

Inventory Accounting: The process of determining the cost of goods held for sale and recording it as an asset until the goods are sold.

Investing Activities: Activities related to acquiring or disposing of long-term assets, such as property, plant, and equipment or investments in other companies.

Journal Entries: The recordings of transactions in a company's accounting records using debits and credits.

Liabilities: Obligations of a business that arise from past transactions and require future sacrifices of economic resources.

Liability Accounts: Accounts that represent the debts or obligations owed by a business, such as accounts payable, loans payable, and accrued expenses.

Liquidity Ratios: Ratios that measure a company's ability to meet its short-term obligations using its current assets.

Loss on Sale: The amount by which the proceeds from the sale of an asset are less than its carrying value.

Operating Activities: Activities related to the day-to-day operations of a business, such as sales, purchases, and expenses.

Periodic Inventory Method: An inventory valuation method that requires a physical count of inventory at the end of the accounting period to determine the cost of goods sold.

Perpetual Inventory Method: A system of tracking inventory in real-time, where the quantity and value of each item are continuously updated as sales and purchases occur.

Profitability Ratios: Financial ratios that measure a company's ability to generate profit relative to its sales, assets, or equity. Examples include gross profit margin, return on assets, and return on equity.

Revenue Accounts: Accounts that record the income earned by a company from its primary business activities, such as sales of goods or services.

Salvage Value: The estimated residual value of an asset at the end of its useful life, which is used to calculate depreciation expenses.

Statement of Retained Earnings: A financial statement that shows the changes in a company's retained earnings over a specific period, including net income or loss, dividends, and adjustments.

Straight-Line Method: A common depreciation method where the cost of an asset is evenly allocated over its estimated useful life.

Trial Balance: A list of all the general ledger accounts and their balances at a specific point in time. It is used to ensure that debit and credit entries are equal and to detect any errors or omissions before preparing financial statements.

T-Accounts: Visual representations of individual general ledger accounts in the form of a "T", with debits on the left side and credits on the right side. They are used to analyze transactions and prepare financial statements.

Units-of-Production Method: A depreciation method that allocates the cost of an asset based on its usage or production output over its useful life. This method is commonly used for assets that wear out or become obsolete based on their usage rather than time.

Made in the USA
Columbia, SC
28 September 2023